## **Shadows that Glimmer in the Ice**

Moonlight dances on the frost,
Casting shadows, never lost.
Whispers softly in the night,
As the world is bathed in light.

Jingle bells and carols ring,
Voices rise, the joy we bring.
Children's laughter, pure delight,
Magical scenes, a lovely sight.

Every corner glows and gleams,
Frosted windows, winter dreams.
Colors sparkling, hearts entwined,
Warmth and cheer are well-defined.

In this wonder, spirits soar,
Every moment, we adore.
Shadows glimmer, soft and nice,
In the stillness of the ice.

## Chill of the Silent Night

Stars twinkle high in the velvet sky,
Laughter and cheer as the snowflakes fly.
Warm fires crackle with stories told,
Hearts aglow in the winter's hold.

Cups of cocoa and marshmallows sweet,
Friends gather close, a festive treat.
Carols echo through the frosty air,
A night of magic, none can compare.

## Whispers in a Winter's Grasp

Gentle snow whispers on streets below,
Twinkling lights set a warm, soft glow.
Families join in a circle tight,
Creating warmth in the frosty night.

With every laughter, a spirit's lift,
Moments treasured, the perfect gift.
Winter's embrace, a comforting sigh,
Together we thrive, beneath the sky.

## Shattered Ice and Silent Echoes

Icicles hang like crystal chandeliers,
Children's laughter dances, brightens fears.
Skates glide swiftly on frozen trails,
In the joyous news, no heart ever fails.

Candles flicker, casting shadows deep,
Memories linger, their warmth we keep.
Celebration sparks from each joyful cheer,
A symphony of love, ringing clear.

## Beneath the Icy Veil

Underneath twinkling stars' embrace,
Sparks of joy illuminate the space.
Frosted branches wear their silver crowns,
In this wonderland, all cares drown.

As carols soar on the chilly breeze,
Hearts entwined, forever at ease.
We gather close as the cold winds sigh,
In the warmth of love, we feel alive.

## Beneath the Layered Silence

Under the stars, laughter floats,
Joyful whispers, spinning hopes.
Bright lights twinkle, spirits soar,
Together we dance, forevermore.

Snowflakes fall, a gentle cheer,
Warm hearts gather, drawing near.
Beneath the moon, our dreams ignite,
In this festive, wondrous night.

## When Frost Kisses the Soul

The world is wrapped in silver lace,
With every breath, we find our place.
Glistening paths, like dreams in tow,
Embracing warmth, our hearts aglow.

Each frosty wind, a joyful song,
Uniting us where we belong.
In the chill, we find delight,
As laughter blooms in the quiet night.

## Dimming Lanterns in the Chill

Lanterns sway in the winter breeze,
Flickering flames, like whispers seize.
Under the boughs, we share our tales,
With each word, our spirit sails.

The night grows deep, the air is bright,
A tapestry of stars in sight.
Cocoa warms our jubilant chats,
As joyous echoes gently spats.

## Heartbeats in the Frozen Hollow

In the hollow, where silence sings,
Heartbeats blend with winter's rings.
Gathered close, we share our dreams,
Creating joy in soft moonbeams.

Every glance, a story spun,
Fireside warmth, we bask in fun.
With every laugh, the chill recedes,
A festive bond, our hearts take lead.

### **Veins of Winter's Breath**

Frost dances on the eaves,
Laughter echoes through the trees.
Twinkling lights adorn the night,
Joy spills forth, pure delight.

Children sledding down the hill,
Snowflakes swirl, the world is still.
Cider brews, a fragrant spell,
In every heart, the warmth does dwell.

Neighbors gather, stories shared,
In this season, no one's spared.
From the hearth, a golden glow,
In winter's breath, love starts to flow.

## Shivers in the Glistening Dark

Moonlight glimmers on the snow,
Each crystal spark a glowing show.
Whispers of frost weave through the night,
In every shadow, there's pure delight.

Stars twinkle like a thousand eyes,
Witness to dreams that softly rise.
Children's laughter fills the air,
Wrapped in warmth, free from care.

Bonfires crackle with a glow,
Faces dance in the undertow.
Hot cocoa shared, spirits lift,
In the dark, we find our gift.

## A Lament for Lost Warmth

Chill winds whisper through the pines,
Memories fade with the bright sun's lines.
Fireplaces hum a lonely song,
Echoes of warmth where we belong.

Stockings hung, but hearts feel bare,
Missing the laughter's soft snare.
Yet in the frost, hope's ember glows,
In every heart, the warmth still flows.

Gathered round with tales to tell,
We share our smiles, despite the chill.
As shadows dance and spirits soar,
In memories warm, we still explore.

**Shadows Beneath the Snow**

Silent whispers in the night,
Shadows twirl in pure moonlight.
Beneath the snow, the world lies thick,
Life's pulse beats, a secret trick.

Branches bending, heavy with white,
Shimmering in the soft twilight.
Embers glow in distant homes,
Inviting souls from where they roam.

Footprints trace a path anew,
Each step speaks of joys accrued.
Underneath the frosty cloak,
In our hearts, warmth still awoke.

## Shadows of a Frozen Moon

Beneath a moon of silver light,
The shadows dance, a merry sight.
Laughter floats on frosty air,
Joy and wonder everywhere.

Children play in snow so bright,
Chasing dreams in pure delight.
Glowing candles line the street,
Warmth and cheer in every beat.

## The Hushed Cries of Winter

Whispers swirl in the crisp night,
Under stars, a twinkling light.
Snowflakes falling, soft and white,
Covering all in purest sight.

Fireplaces crackle, glow aglow,
Friends gather near, spirits flow.
With every cheer and every song,
In winter's arms, we all belong.

## **Cold Embrace of Dusk**

The twilight fades, a gentle sigh,
As colors blend, the night draws nigh.
In the chill, we find a place,
Where laughter melts the icy space.

Bundled close, we share our tales,
The warmth of hearts, as night prevails.
Under the stars, our spirits soar,
In the cold, we crave for more.

## Echoes in the Frosted Air

Echoes ring through frosted trees,
Carried gently on the breeze.
Songs of joy fill the night sky,
Underneath the twinkling high.

Frosted windows, a glowing glow,
Homes alive with warmth and flow.
Together we cherish, together we sing,
In the heart of winter, love takes wing.

## Constellations of Ice and Sorrow

Under the stars, ice crystals gleam,
Whispers of joy in a frosty dream.
Laughter dances on the chilly breeze,
Melodies wrap around like the trees.

Candles flicker in the wintry night,
Every heart glows with warm delight.
Sorrow melts under moon's gentle glow,
In constellations of love, we grow.

## Treading Softly on Frozen Soil

Footprints mark paths on the crisp white ground,
Soft echoes of laughter, a sweet, joyous sound.
Beneath the frost, life quietly waits,
As hope blooms anew through winter's gates.

Snowflakes flutter like confetti in flight,
Children's giggles ring out in the night.
Treading softly, we cherish the chill,
With hearts bound in warmth, we seek the thrill.

# The Cold Touch of Yesterday

Memories linger, like snow on the pines,
The chill of the past in soft, silver lines.
Yet laughter resounds through the shadows of time,
In the echoes of joy, our spirits climb.

With each breath, the past fades away,
Hope paints tomorrow in bright shades of gray.
The cold touch of yesterday, bittersweet,
Yet love's glowing fire makes our hearts meet.

## In the Hush of Winter's Breath

Silence wraps around like a tender shawl,
In winter's hush, we hear the call.
Whispers of magic float on the air,
As celebration lingers everywhere.

Stars twinkle above in the velvety night,
Smiles illuminate hearts, pure and bright.
In the hush of winter, joy finds its way,
In every snowflake, a promise of play.

## The Icebound Heart's Lament

In the glow of a flickering flame,
Winter's chill takes a playful aim.
Laughter echoes through the frost,
In this wonderland, we count not the cost.

Snowflakes dance like whispers soft,
Underneath the branches, lofty and oft.
With every twirl, the spirits gleam,
Creating magic, a shared dream.

Fires crackle, and hearts ignite,
Around the hearth, we find delight.
With friends and cheer, the night feels bright,
In this festival, all wrongs feel right.

## **Nightfall's Decaying Breath**

Stars emerge in garments white,
Spreading joy throughout the night.
Beneath the sky, a stillness found,
In silence, ancient truths abound.

Glow of lanterns, a warm embrace,
Every corner, a smiling face.
As shadows dance, they celebrate,
Chasing away the heavy weight.

The air is thick with festive songs,
Where everyone truly belongs.
In whispered tales, we find our thread,
Binding hearts, where love has spread.

## Fallen Leaves of Permafrost

Crunching underfoot, a crisp delight,
Nature's artwork in vibrant light.
Golden hues in the frosty air,
Gathered friends, a colorful flare.

Pumpkin treats and sweetened spice,
With every laugh, we pay the price.
For memories made in the falling leaves,
Joy and warmth, our heart believes.

Winds whistle tunes of old and new,
In this revelry, we bloom anew.
Embracing the chill with open arms,
In fleeting days, we find our charms.

## Beneath the White Shroud

Blankets of snow in the silent night,
A festive spirit takes its flight.
In the hush, there's a whisper clear,
Delight and wonder, drawing near.

Children's laughter, a lively sound,
As footprints trace joy on the ground.
With every mitten and frosted sigh,
Together we watch the moon climb high.

From rooftops adorned with twinkling glow,
Spreading warmth in the depths of snow.
A chorus rising, all hearts entwined,
In this magic, true peace we find.

## Imprints of Lost Whispers

In a hall where laughter rings,
Echoes dance on vibrant wings,
The stars above, a twinkling sight,
Celebrate the joy of night.

Beneath the glow of lanterns bright,
Old tales weave in soft moonlight,
Each whisper holds a charming tune,
A gathering where hearts attune.

The music flows, serene and free,
As shadows sway in harmony,
In every smile, a story spun,
Together, we are all as one.

## The Veil of Time in Frozen Moments

Beneath the boughs of frosted trees,
A shimmer glows upon the breeze,
Winter's magic wraps us tight,
Transforming day, igniting night.

Snowflakes dance in twinkling light,
Creating a dreamlike sight,
In cozy nooks, with friends we bask,
In the warmth of joy, we dare to ask.

With every laugh, a moment glows,
Time stands still as friendship flows,
In frozen frames, our hearts do swell,
In this embrace, all is well.

## **Wandering Through Crystal Dreams**

Step lightly where the shadows play,
In a realm where visions sway,
Canvas skies of azure hues,
Awaken dreams we dare to choose.

Underneath the starlit veils,
Adventures weave in whispered tales,
Each twinkling light a guiding friend,
In this dance, the joy won't end.

Chasing colors through the night,
Hearts ignited in sheer delight,
With every breath, the magic blooms,
In crystal realms, the spirit zooms.

## Reverie in a Hibernal Glade

In shaded groves where silence reigns,
The winter hush softly gains,
A tapestry of dreams unfolds,
In the heart, the warmth it holds.

Fires crackle with a gentle cheer,
As stories linger, crystal clear,
Footprints left in snow's embrace,
In these moments, we find our place.

The world outside stands still and bright,
While cozy hearts embrace the night,
With every sip and laugh we share,
The hibernal glade becomes our fair.

## Whispers of the Icebound

In the glow of twilight's embrace,
Snowflakes twirl, a soft lace.
Laughter dances on the chilly air,
As joy unfolds everywhere.

The stars above begin to gleam,
Casting dreams in a frosty stream.
Children play with shining eyes,
Beneath the frost-kissed, velvet skies.

Muffled music from houses near,
Spirits rise, none to fear.
The icebound whispers, secrets told,
Of warmth and cheer in the cold.

Together we gather, hearts so bright,
Under the stars, a magnificent sight.
Hand in hand, we heed the call,
In the festival's magic, we give our all.

## Specters Beneath the Glaze

A shimmer wraps the world tonight,
All adorned in silver light.
Ghostly figures glide and sway,
In the fields where children play.

Beneath the glaze, a story spun,
Of laughter shared and hours fun.
Candles flicker with soft delight,
Guiding souls through wintry night.

The whispers of the ancient trees,
Echoing hopes on the frosty breeze.
Crisp and clear, the air so bright,
As heartbeats dance in pure delight.

We toast to dreams and midnight cheers,
As time melts softly, erasing fears.
In the shadows, love will blaze,
With specters bright beneath the glaze.

## Treading Softly on Bitter Ground

In the hush of snowflakes falling,
Softly, gently, the night is calling.
Footsteps leave their fleeting trace,
In this wintry, magical space.

The chill wraps round like a tender hug,
While warmth ignites a joyful tug.
Mirthful echoes fill the air,
As hearts unite in vibrant flair.

Fires crackle with stories shared,
In the glow, no soul is scared.
Treading lightly on this ground,
We find love lost and joy profound.

And as the evening stars do gleam,
We drift together in a dream.
On bitter paths, we find our way,
In festive moments, let us stay.

## The Lament of Wintry Solitude

As twilight falls in silence deep,
A wintry lament begins to creep.
Soft echoes of dreams long past,
In solitude's grip, shadows cast.

Yet within this chilly embrace,
Lies a spark of a warm, bright space.
Where we gather, hearts entwined,
In laughter shared and joy defined.

Through the frost, a chorus sings,
Hope rises with the joy it brings.
Winter's chill, a bittersweet tune,
Transforming night into a boon.

So let us weave this night anew,
With threads of laughter, skies so blue.
For in the heart of solitude,
We find the balm of festive mood.

## Echoes of the Shivering Pines

Beneath the stars, the pines sway,
Whispers of joy in frosty play.
Laughter rings through winter's night,
As candles flicker, warm and bright.

Snowflakes dance in silver glows,
Every heart a tale bestows.
The scent of pine and fire's light,
Together weave a perfect sight.

Children splash in pure white snow,
Building dreams where cold winds blow.
Echoes of cheer fill the air,
Wrapped in magic beyond compare.

Raise a glass, let spirits soar,
For every heart can sing once more.
In the embrace of winter's grace,
We find our joy in this sweet place.

## Frozen Phantoms and Whispered Pines

In the silence, shadows glide,
Frozen phantoms, winter's pride.
Underneath the moon's soft gaze,
Whispered secrets through the haze.

Echoes linger, soft and clear,
Memories of those we hold dear.
Joy and laughter, dance and play,
In the crisp embrace of day.

Firelight flickers, spirits rise,
As stars twinkle in snowy skies.
Hand in hand, we brave the cold,
Sharing stories, warm and bold.

Together we weave a bright dream,
In winter's chill, our hearts redeem.
For in the cold, we find our path,
A festive dance, our simple wrath.

## Dreams Entombed in the Snow

Beneath the blanket, soft and white,
Dreams entombed, hidden from sight.
A world transformed, pure and bright,
In winter's grasp, we find delight.

Footprints mark a winding trail,
In laughter's wake, we shall not fail.
Childlike wonder fills our eyes,
As snowflakes twirl from wintry skies.

Around the fire, stories flow,
Of distant lands where warm winds blow.
But here we share, both deep and light,
In dreams entombed, our hearts take flight.

Raise a cheer for winter's grace,
As joy and love fill every space.
In frosted air, a festive cheer,
Together we make memories dear.

## The Mirage of Frost

Glimmers of ice on branches fine,
The mirage of frost, a sparkling line.
Each breath a cloud on the chilly air,
Festive spirits rise without a care.

Chimes of laughter echo through,
As children skate on the frozen hue.
A tapestry woven, bright and bold,
In the miracle of winter's hold.

Fireside whispers, warm and clear,
As tales unfold, loved ones near.
In every twinkle, joy ignites,
Creating memories on coldest nights.

Raise your voice, let the carols ring,
For in winter's heart, we're meant to sing.
In this mirage, we find our place,
Spirits uplifted in winter's grace.

## Dusk of the Crystal World

The sun dips low, a golden hue,
Sparkling crystals come into view.
Laughter dances in the crisp, cool air,
Joyful hearts, free from care.

Twinkling lights ignite the night,
Children's faces gleam with delight.
A world transformed, a wondrous sight,
In the dusk of the crystal world, so bright.

Frosty breath in the evening chill,
Every moment, a memory to fill.
Sing out loud, let spirits soar,
In this magical place, we want for more.

Under starlit skies, friendships unite,
Gathered together, warm and tight.
In fleeting time, let joy abound,
As we revel in the crystal ground.

## Harbingers of Ice

Winter whispers in the gentle breeze,
Icicles hang from the swaying trees.
Joyous songs weave through the air,
As laughter floats without a care.

Snowflakes dance, a shimmering quilt,
Every heart, with warmth, is built.
Fires crackle, their glow so bright,
In the harbingers of ice, pure delight.

Glistening paths where footprints tell,
Of merry moments and stories to swell.
With every cheer, the night ignites,
In the tapestry of winter nights.

So raise a glass to the frosty cheer,
With friends and family gathered near.
In the embrace of winter's grace,
Let joy's melody find its place.

## Chasing Shadows on Glacial Ground

In twilight's glow, we roam the night,
With shadows chasing in silver light.
The world aglow in frosty white,
A festive dream, our hearts take flight.

Laughter echoes, crisp and clear,
As we gather, holding dear.
With every cheer, the cold subsides,
In this moment, joy abides.

Tracks in snow, a trail we leave,
In the glacial ground, we believe.
Together woven, our stories blend,
In the chase of shadows, without end.

Eager hearts, the world aglow,
Under the moon, our spirits flow.
For in the cold, we find our sound,
Chasing shadows on glacial ground.

## The Heart Beneath a Layer of Frost

Beneath the ice, a warmth does dwell,
In every heart, a tale to tell.
With each soft laugh, the air ignites,
In the winter's chill, we find our lights.

Snowflakes twirl in a wild ballet,
While friends unite to catch the sway.
With cups raised high, we share our cheer,
In this season, all draw near.

Frosted windows, warm inside,
Through azure skies, our dreams collide.
In every moment, memories bloom,
In the heart beneath the layer of frost, there's room.

So let us gather, hand in hand,
Dancing lightly on winter's land.
As laughter rings through the joyous air,
The heart beneath, forever rare.

## **Dusk's Icy Caress**

As dusk descends with a frosty grace,
Twinkling lights adorn each space.
Laughter dances in the crisp night air,
Hearts are warm, it's a time to share.

Snowflakes swirl in a joyful flight,
Creating magic in the soft twilight.
Families gather, stories unfold,
In the embrace of winter's hold.

Fires crackle in the distance bright,
Casting shadows that twinkle with light.
Mirth and cheer in each joyous sigh,
As stars awaken in the navy sky.

With mugs of cocoa and spirits high,
We raise our glasses, letting worries fly.
In dusk's embrace, we feel alive,
To cherish moments where joy will thrive.

## Wraiths of the Winter Chill

Wraiths of winter glide through trees,
Whispers carried on the gentle breeze.
With every flake, a tale is spun,
Of frosty nights and bright winter sun.

Chill in the air, but warmth in our hearts,
As holiday spirit unites all parts.
Revelers gather, a vibrant throng,
In the tapestry of winter's song.

Dancing shadows in the silvered light,
Under the moon, everything feels right.
Joyful voices blend in sweet refrain,
Binding us through the winter's gain.

Together we build, and together we play,
Wraiths of the winter won't lead us astray.
In every snowball and each frosted breath,
We find our warmth in the dance of death.

## Echoes of a Frosted Heart

Echoes linger where love took flight,
Frosted beats twinkling in the night.
Each laughter shared, a joyous sound,
In magic moments, our souls unbound.

Winter's kiss on the cheek so bright,
A reminder of cheer in the darkest night.
Snowy paths where we used to roam,
Bring the heart back to its cherished home.

Gifts of warmth wrapped up with care,
Tell a tale of hearts laid bare.
Together under the starry dome,
In echoes soft, we find our home.

From frosted dawn to night's sweet end,
We weave our dreams, together we mend.
In every whisper of the chill that starts,
Lies the promise of a frost-kissed heart.

### Shadows in the Glistening Snow

Shadows flicker in the glistening snow,
As festive lights put on a show.
Steps are hushed in the pristine white,
Magic pulses through the starry night.

Candles dance in the frosty air,
Glistening streams of joy everywhere.
Children's laughter, a merry tune,
Weaving warmth beneath the moon.

Gathered close around the fire,
Fuelling spirits that never tire.
Glances shared, a kindred spark,
As shadows deepen in the dark.

With hearts alight, we stand so near,
Embracing winter, shedding fear.
Through shadows cast and glimmering glow,
We find our bliss in the falling snow.

## Whispers in the Crystal Twilight

In the dusk where shadows play,
Laughter dances, bright and gay.
Stars awaken, twinkling bright,
Whispers fill the crystal night.

Joyful echoes in the air,
Friendship blooms, beyond compare.
Snowflakes twirl in gentle glee,
As hearts unite, wild and free.

Mirth and warmth in every glance,
Underneath the moon's soft dance.
Happiness in every song,
Together where we all belong.

With every cheer, with every turn,
In this twilight, our spirits burn.
The world aglow, a tapestry,
Of love and joy, eternally.

## Chilled Breath of the Moonlit Veil

Underneath the moonlit veil,
Frosty whispers tell a tale.
Glistening pathways call us near,
Where joy and laughter persevere.

Joyful faces, bright and bold,
As warmth and cheer we'll unfold.
Chilled breaths mingle in the air,
Together, hearts beyond compare.

Songbirds serenade the night,
With melodies that feel so right.
Bright lanterns twinkle in delight,
A festive scene, a pure invite.

In every glance, there's magic found,
In every laugh, a joyful sound.
Together here, we weave a dream,
In moonlit magic, we all beam.

## Lament of the Frozen Woods

In the woods where silence sings,
Lament echoes of lost things.
Frozen branches reach for sky,
Shivering whispers floating by.

Yet beneath the icy layer,
Hopeful hearts begin to stir.
Gathered round the flickering light,
We share warmth on this cold night.

Songs of yore through branches glide,
Memories lost, but hearts abide.
In this frost, we make a start,
Binding souls, both close and far.

Together we'll embrace the chill,
Finding warmth in every thrill.
Lament turns to joy, we see,
In the frozen woods, we're free.

## Shadows in the Glacial Twilight

In shadows where the twilight gleams,
The world awakens, sparking dreams.
Beneath the ice, the whispers play,
In glacial realms, we find our way.

With every step, the echoes hum,
A festive tune, a joyful drum.
Lights entwine in starry grace,
As smiles bloom on every face.

Warm drinks shared in cozy nooks,
Glances warm like cherished books.
With laughter bright, we weave the night,
In frozen air, our spirits flight.

Together we embrace the sway,
In shadows where the children play.
Celebration fills the skies,
In glacial twilight, love never dies.

## The Stillness Between Heartbeats


In the hush of soft delight,
Laughter dances, hearts take flight.
Bubbles rise in evening air,
Joyful moments, free of care.

Candles flicker, shadows play,
As friends gather round to sway.
Songs of cheer fill up the night,
In our hearts, a warm light.

Colors clash, confetti rains,
Life bursts forth in vibrant chains.
Spirit sparkles, spirits soar,
Wishes made and dreams to score.

In the stillness, love amplifies,
Promises heard beneath the skies.
Together here, we celebrate,
In this moment, we create.

## In the Arms of Winter's Twilight

Snowflakes twirl in the fading glow,
Whispers of warmth in the winds that blow.
Fires crackle, tales unfold,
Hearths aglow, and hearts of gold.

Scarves wrapped tight, cheeks so bright,
Glimmers of hope in the chilly night.
Laughter echoes over the snow,
In winter's arms, our spirits grow.

Twinkling lights on branches sway,
Underneath, we dance and play.
Cocoa warms our hands so dear,
In this embrace, there's naught to fear.

Memories made like snowflakes fall,
Together we rise, we heed the call.
In winter's twilight, love ignites,
A festive spirit, pure delights.

## Haunting Ghosts of the Frigid Past

The echoes float on icy breeze,
Whispers of sorrows, haunting pleas.
Yet candle flames carve shadows bright,
Reviving warmth in starry night.

Beneath the moon's soft, silver glow,
Ghosts of laughter begin to flow.
We raise a glass to all that's lost,
In reunion, we pay the cost.

Heritage wrapped in frosty air,
Tales of old, with joy and care.
Each memory a shimmering star,
Guiding us from near and far.

Beneath frost's chill, hearts entwine,
Remembered love, a cherished sign.
In festive revel, we reclaim,
The ghosts that whisper, but bring no shame.

## Beneath the Weight of Winter's Veil

The world adorned in white and gray,
Under winter's gentle sway.
With the frost come dreams so bright,
Shining through the longest night.

Gather close, the fire burns,
In its glow, a heart that yearns.
Cider steams in frosted mugs,
Wraps us warm in cozy hugs.

Sleds and laughter fill the scene,
Glistening like jewels, so serene.
Carols sung with joyous cheer,
Unite us all, the end is near.

Beneath the weight, we shed our fears,
In this moment, laughter steers.
As winter's veil enfolds us tight,
We bask in love, our hearts ignite.

## The Melody of Ruthless Uncertainty

In the air, a song is bright,
Twinkling stars, a dance of light.
Whispers of dreams, they fill the night,
Fleeting joy, a heart's delight.

Laughter echoes through the trees,
Carried gently by the breeze.
Joyous spirits, wild and free,
Chasing shadows, can't you see?

Colors burst like fireworks high,
Filling hearts that learn to fly.
Moments cherished, never shy,
In this fest, let worries die.

Raise a glass, let spirits soar,
Every heartbeat begs for more.
With a cheer, we all explore,
This melody we can't ignore.

## Reflections in the Frosted Glass

Snowflakes dance on windows wide,
In this warmth, we'll all abide.
Mirrored laughter, glow inside,
Hearts entwined, with love as guide.

Candles flicker, stories shared,
Hope and joy, we are prepared.
Sparkling eyes, the room ensnared,
Memories built, none impaired.

Outside world, a glimmer dim,
Within us flows a joyful hymn.
Each reflection, a chance not slim,
Together, we will never brim.

Festive cheer, we celebrate,
In this moment, love's our fate.
Raise your voice, it's never late,
Together, let our hearts create.

## **Beneath a Blanket of Silence**

Softly falls the gentle snow,
Wrapping all in purest glow.
Quiet moments, whispers slow,
In this peace, our spirits grow.

Fires crackle, warmth inside,
Hearts alight as love's our guide.
Shared stories, where hopes abide,
This embrace, we won't decide.

Candles bright, with glowing smiles,
Time slips by, yet here we'll stay.
With each laugh, our joy compiles,
Binding us in this sweet play.

Beneath the silence, love is found,
In cherished moments, hearts unbound.
Celebrate the joy around,
In silence, our hopes resound.

## Grieving the Withered Green

Leaves once bright now fade away,
Nature's song, a somber play.
Yet in change, we find the way,
Growing hope in colors gray.

Fields once lush, now bare and meek,
But within, a strength we seek.
Through the dark, our hearts can speak,
In the silence, love's unique.

Remembering the vibrant days,
Yet embracing new heart's ways.
With every tear, we mend the frays,
Finding light in life's arrays.

Grieving shifts to gentle grace,
Life renews in every space.
Withered green, we still embrace,
In the cycle, joy we trace.

## Echoes of the Glistening Veil

Frosted whispers in the night,
Laughter dances, pure delight.
Under stars that brightly gleam,
Magic flows like a waking dream.

Glittering paths of snowy lace,
Every heart finds its warm place.
Joyful voices fill the air,
In this moment, none compare.

Candles flicker, shadows play,
Warming spirits on display.
Together we will raise a cheer,
For love and joy are gathered here.

### The Last Ember in a Shell of Ice

In winter's cradle, embers glow,
A festive warmth in the cold below.
Joyful hearts ignite the night,
Whispers dancing, spirits bright.

Ice draped branches, glistening white,
With every laugh, our souls take flight.
Together we share this sacred space,
Embracing life in a warm embrace.

Hand in hand, we spin and sway,
Wrapping memories, come what may.
The last ember, a glowing star,
Reminding us just how blessed we are.

## Dance of the Frozen Willow

Beneath the willow, spirits twirl,
In frosty air, we laugh and whirl.
Snowflakes shimmering in the light,
A tapestry of pure delight.

Glistening branches, a silvery crown,
Every whisper a joyful sound.
In the arms of the night, we sway,
Celebrating the warmth of day.

Candied treats and bright array,
In our hearts, the music plays.
Together as one, the world we greet,
At the frozen willow, we feel complete.

## Glimpses Through the Wintry Veil

Peeking through the frosty pane,
Glowing lights that dance like rain.
Every moment filled with cheer,
Special memories gathering near.

A blanket soft, the world at rest,
In this stillness, we are blessed.
Laughter echoes, stories shared,
In this warmth, we're all prepared.

Glimpses of joy through the haze,
In the winter's sparkling glaze.
Together we'll revel in delight,
Crafting dreams 'neath the shimmering night.

## Secrets Linger in the Chill

Whispers dance in frosty air,
Laughter rings, a joyous flare.
Families gather, hearts entwine,
While twinkling lights above do shine.

Mittens snug, and cocoa warm,
Each little joy, a sweet, soft charm.
Snowflakes kiss the smiling ground,
In every corner, warmth is found.

Children play with glee and cheer,
Building dreams of winter's sphere.
A symphony of bells and song,
In this festive night, we all belong.

Glistening stars in velvet skies,
Paint the world with bright surprise.
Secrets linger, spirits bright,
In winter's hug, love takes flight.

## Beneath the Frigid Moon

Underneath the silver glow,
Footprints trace in purest snow.
Stars above like diamonds gleam,
Spreading warmth, a shared dream.

Fires crackle, stories flow,
Families gather, spirits grow.
Laughter mingles with the chill,
Creating bonds that time can't kill.

Pine trees clothed in frosted white,
Candle flames flicker, oh so bright.
Beneath the frigid moon's embrace,
We find our warmth in love's sweet grace.

Melodies of joy take flight,
Filling hearts with pure delight.
In unity, our voices rise,
As festive cheer lights up the skies.

## Sighs of the Wintry Apparition

Phantoms dance in frosty air,
Spirits weave without a care.
Softly glows the winter night,
Whispers echo, pure delight.

Blankets warm wrapped snugly tight,
Under dim, enchanting light.
The wintry apparition sighs,
As wonder sparks in children's eyes.

Frosty branches gently sway,
In the hush of this sweet stay.
Magic woven into time,
Can we hear the chime of rhyme?

Invisible hands paint the scene,
Creating joy that feels so keen.
With every sigh, our hearts rejoice,
In the night, we find our voice.

### A Canvas of White and Woe

Blanket of snow, a canvas wide,
Concealing all that lies inside.
Children build their dreams anew,
While laughter echoes, soft and true.

In this frame of wintry peace,
Moments dance, our cares release.
Joy unfolds with every flake,
As the world begins to wake.

Candles flicker, shadows play,
Whispers of love in soft array.
In the chill, our warmth ignites,
A kaleidoscope of festive lights.

Yet beneath the gleam and glow,
Lies a heart that longs to grow.
Each snowflake tells a tale of old,
In this canvas, life unfolds.

## Portraits of a Crystal Night

Stars twinkle like gems, radiant and bright,
The world wrapped in silver, pure delight.
Caroling voices float through the air,
In the embrace of joy, we find our share.

Snowflakes dance down, a magical sight,
Bright lanterns shining, banishing night.
Laughter of children, spirits set free,
In the warmth of the hearth, together we'll be.

Mittens and scarves, colors abound,
Underneath the clear skies, love's melody found.
With each joyful step, we wander and roam,
Creating our memories, we feel at home.

So, raise a glass high, let the cheer grow,
For this crystal night, we let our hearts glow.
Together we gather, friends old and new,
In the magic of winter, happiness too.

# The Quiet Thaw

Spring whispers softly, a sweet serenade,
In thawing arms, winter's grip starts to fade.
Buds peep from slumber, life begins to sing,
In the heart of the earth, we celebrate spring.

Streams bubbling gently, laughter in sound,
Emerging from silence, life's rhythm is found.
Sunlight spills gold on the thawing ground,
Each moment a treasure, joy all around.

Children all dancing in fields lush and green,
In nature's revival, a magical scene.
With hearts open wide, we welcome the light,
In the quiet thaw, everything feels right.

So gather together, let spirits take flight,
Embrace the new season, bask in its light.
For in every thaw, there's hope to be sought,
In the blooms of tomorrow, joy can't be bought.

## Underneath the Winter's Grief

Beneath the frost, a longing stirs deep,
Quietly waiting, the world drifts to sleep.
Yet in the stillness, a hope starts to grow,
Underneath the winter, spring's whispers will flow.

As snow blankets all, there's beauty to find,
In the trees' icy branches, artistry kind.
A moment of magic, in silence we tread,
Finding warmth in the dreams that dance in our head.

Each breath of the cold, a reminder so sweet,
That life reawakens, with each heartbeat.
Gathered together by fires that gleam,
Underneath winter's grief, we cherish our dream.

So let the winds howl, let the snowflakes whirl,
In the glow of the hearth, see the joy unfurl.
For even in sadness, we find a retreat,
Underneath winter's grief, the warmth is complete.

## Chilled Memories in Twilight

The sky blushes pink as the day softly fades,
With whispers of twilight, where magic invades.
Chilled memories linger, frozen in time,
In the shimmer of dusk, all feels so sublime.

Footprints in snow trace the laughter of old,
With stories and secrets in silence retold.
Through the frosty air, a chill so inviting,
In the glow of the evening, there's warmth igniting.

Gathered 'round fires, with courage we share,
In each glowing ember, we're letting down care.
Candles flicker gently, casting soft light,
Chilled memories captured, a beautiful sight.

So hold onto these moments, let joy intertwine,
As twilight embraces, our hearts are aligned.
In the stillness of night, we cherish this gift,
Chilled memories in twilight, together we lift.

### **Veils of Winter's Grasp**

Snowflakes twirl like dancers, bright,
Each sparkling twinkling in the light.
Laughter echoes, cheers arise,
Underneath the starry skies.

Warmth of hearts in scarves wrapped tight,
Joyful songs take flight tonight.
Candles glow with gentle sway,
In this festive, frosty play.

Tree adorned with silver charm,
Embers crackle, keep us warm.
Whispers of the season's cheer,
Gather friends and loved ones near.

Festive feasts and playful sights,
Dancing shadows, warm delights.
Veils of winter, pure and bold,
In joyous arms, our tales unfold.

## Ghosts Beneath the Snow

Hushed whispers roam in winter's breath,
Echoes of laughter, hints of theft.
Footprints trace a frosty ground,
Memories of joy abound.

Beneath the layers, spirits gleam,
In shimmering white, they softly beam.
Decorated trees, a dazzling show,
Ghosts of laughter beneath the snow.

Carols drift through the crisp night air,
As families gather, love to share.
Hot cocoa warms the waiting hands,
In this wonder, our heart expands.

With each soft crunch beneath our feet,
Friendly ghosts, we joyfully greet.
Beneath the snow, a magic flow,
Celebrations warm, despite the cold.

## Shattered Light on Icy Paths

Crystals shatter in the morning glow,
Icy paths where laughter flows.
Fragile dreams in the sun's embrace,
Festive shimmers fill our space.

Footsteps dance on silver trails,
Joyful spirits, laughter prevails.
Every blink a story spun,
Underneath the warming sun.

Scarves wrapped tight, we twirl and leap,
In chilly air, our secrets keep.
With every cheer, the world ignites,
Shattered light on wondrous nights.

Together we weave this magical thread,
With every joke, our smiles spread.
Brighter days in wintry strains,
Joy unfolds as silence wanes.

## **Frosted Dreams in the Silent Grove**

Beneath the boughs, in frosted sheen,
Whispers linger, soft and keen.
Every branch a tale to spin,
In nature's hush, our joys begin.

Sparkling twinkles on the leaves,
Gifts of wonder, magic weaves.
Snowflakes flutter, dreams take flight,
In the grove, all hearts feel light.

Candles flicker in the dark,
New friendships bloom, igniting spark.
Around the fire, stories flow,
Frosted dreams in the silent glow.

Winter's cloak, a gentle balm,
United voices bring sweet calm.
In every heart, a vibrant song,
Together, where we all belong.

## Solitary Paths Through Fading Light

Beneath the orange glow we stride,
With laughter echoing wide and free.
The whispers of the woods confide,
In twilight's dance, sweet joy to see.

Candles flicker in the dusk,
As shadows play upon the ground.
Our hearts are full, and spirits brisk,
In festive tune, a love profound.

Majestic pines in coats of white,
Stand guard as stars begin their show.
We journey forth, in pure delight,
Through paths where visions softly flow.

The night unfolds, a velvet cloak,
While holiday tales are spun anew.
A song that sings, the fire stokes,
In solitude, we find our view.

## Where Light Meets Ice

In crystalline silence, moments gleam,
As streetlights cast their playful glow.
Children's laughter hangs like a dream,
In the frigid air, sweet joys bestow.

Sparkling jewels on branches sway,
Nature's canvas, stark yet bright.
Every turn feels like a play,
Where festivity sprinkles light.

Skaters twirl on frozen lakes,
In graceful arcs, the chill embraced.
The world awakes, and cheer awakes,
In this realm, our hearts find place.

Voices join in merry song,
Under the magic, lives intertwine.
Here, where light and ice belong,
Moments linger, rich and fine.

## The Hidden Depths of Winter

Beneath the surface, warmth does hide,
As snowflakes blanket all we see.
In quiet corners, joy abides,
The pulse of life, a mystery.

A cozy hearth with stories told,
Lifts spirits high, dispels the gloom.
With mugs of cocoa, hearts unfold,
In laughter's glow, we find our room.

As twilight paints the skies with grace,
Each star ignites the velvet night.
In whispered dreams, we find our place,
Where winter's hold turns soft and light.

Beneath the frost, a warmth does dwell,
In smiles exchanged as memories bloom.
In hidden depths, we weave our spell,
Amidst the chill, a festive room.

## **Last Embrace of Autumn**

The leaves cascade in vibrant hues,
A final dance before the fall.
Beneath the boughs, the earth renews,
As nature sings her last enthrall.

Pumpkins glow with candlelight,
While harvest feasts adorn the table.
In every heart, the warmth ignites,
Together, strong and ever stable.

Fires crackle as stories blend,
With friends around, our spirits soar.
In this embrace, the seasons mend,
Carving memories to adore.

As autumn bows, the chill creeps near,
A bittersweet farewell it brings.
Yet joy will linger, soft and clear,
In heartfelt tunes, the spirit swings.

## The Frost That Seals Our Words

In winter's breath, the laughter glows,
With every smile, our spirits rose.
The chill is sweet, as joy declares,
Amidst the frost, the love we share.

The night is bright with twinkling lights,
As carols echo through the nights.
Together we stand, hearts entwined,
In this warm embrace, so well-defined.

Snowflakes dance, as dreams take flight,
In this festive peace, all feels right.
With cocoa warm and fireside cheer,
We gather close, our friends all near.

So let us toast to moments bright,
To laughter shared on this joyful night.
The frost may seal our whispered words,
But love's warmth thrives, as magic stirs.

## A Haunting in the Starlit Cold

Beneath the moon's pale, silver gaze,
The stars align in festive ways.
Whispers of old, they fill the air,
With secrets wrapped, a ghostly flare.

The frost, it glimmers, a spectral sight,
As shadows dance with pure delight.
Echoes sing of frosty glee,
In the chill, our hearts are free.

Through branches bare, the lanterns glow,
Guiding our steps through the white snow.
In each soft gust, a story told,
A haunting tune in the starlit cold.

Together we laugh, as spirits sway,
Finding joy in the night's ballet.
With every breath, the magic's spun,
In this enchanted world, we're all as one.

## Silhouettes in the Pale Array

In the soft glow of twilight's hue,
Silhouettes dance, as hope breaks through.
Festive hearts in a shining throng,
We sway together, a jubilant song.

Under draping lights, we share a smile,
In every moment, we linger a while.
The winter air, it sparkles bright,
With every twinkle, we chase the night.

Frost on branches, a delicate lace,
In this festive land, we find our place.
With laughter rising, our worries fade,
In joyous circles, memories made.

So let us celebrate with cheer so bold,
In colors of warmth, this season unfolds.
Through every shadow that we perceive,
Together we stand, in love, we believe.

## Beneath the Surface of the Ice

Beneath the frost, a world concealed,
In icy depths, our dreams revealed.
With every laugh and twinkling eye,
We raise our voices to the sky.

In raucous joy, the echoes play,
As festive hearts make winter sway.
The lights above, they flicker bright,
Guiding us through the starlit night.

Together we dance, with spirits high,
Feeling the warmth as snowflakes fly.
In this embrace, we find our peace,
With every heartbeat, our joys increase.

So let the cold bring us together,
In laughter shared, not just the weather.
Beneath the surface, our love will rise,
As endless joy lights up the skies.

## Hidden Secrets in the Frost

Glistening crystals dance in light,
Whispers of magic fill the night.
Underneath the cold moon's glow,
Hidden secrets start to flow.

Paths of silver through the trees,
Swaying gently in the breeze.
Every shadow holds a tale,
Of winter's charm and frost's veil.

Laughter echoes, pure delight,
Friends are gathered, hearts feel light.
With every twinkle, warmth ignites,
Creating joy on frosty nights.

As we gather 'round the fire,
The spirit sparks, our hearts aspire.
In this frosty, festive cheer,
We celebrate, we hold so dear.

## **Where the Wild Things Shiver**

Amid the woods where spirits play,
Wild things shiver, come what may.
Frosty breath, a chill in air,
Calling all to join the fair.

Beneath the boughs of ancient trees,
Laughter dances with the breeze.
Every heartbeat resonates,
With winter's magic that awaits.

Candles glow in softest light,
Guiding paths through wintry night.
In the hush, a festive cheer,
Bringing joy to those held dear.

Snowflakes swirl like dreams untold,
In this world where hearts are bold.
Together, we embrace the chill,
Finding warmth in love's sweet thrill.

## Beneath the Whispering Snow

Beneath the whispering snow so bright,
Softly falling, pure delight.
Every flake a tiny star,
Carrying wishes from afar.

Gathered close, around the fire,
Voices lifted, we inspire.
Stories shared of dreams and cheer,
Filling hearts with warmth sincere.

Sparkling eyes, a twinkle here,
In this moment, love draws near.
Holding hands, we dance and sing,
Celebrating what warmth can bring.

Beyond the drifts of silent night,
Fests abound in purest light.
From frozen ground to sky above,
In winter's heart, we share our love.

## Shards of Light on the Frozen Lake

On frozen lakes where shadows play,
Shards of light dance in the spray.
Glowing hues of blues and gold,
Winter's magic, stories told.

Skaters glide as laughter rings,
Frosty breath, oh, what joy brings!
Chasing dreams on icy glass,
Moments cherished, none shall pass.

Underneath the evening sky,
With every twirl, our spirits fly.
Hot cocoa shared, in warmth we bask,
In this magic, no need to ask.

As starlit skies begin to shine,
In this moment, we feel divine.
Together in this festive dance,
Finding joy in winter's trance.

## When the World Turned to Glass

When the world turned to glass, we danced with delight,
Shimmering fragments that glistened so bright.
Joy spread like sunlight, warming the night,
In this festival moment, everything felt right.

Laughter echoed in the cool evening air,
As twinkling lights adorned every square.
With each sparkling shimmer, we twirled without care,
In a magical setting, love was everywhere.

Time seemed to linger in starlit embrace,
A canvas of dreams painted soft on our face.
With each festive heartbeat, we found our own place,
In the beauty of moments, our worries erased.

So let the world shatter, let glasses collide,
In the spirit of joy, let our hearts be our guide.
For when the world turned, we stood side by side,
In a celebration of life, where love won't subside.

## A Symphony of Cold and Silence

In a symphony of cold, the silence took flight,
Snowflakes twirling softly, a dance of pure white.
With each frosty whisper, the world felt just right,
As we gathered together, wrapped warm and tight.

Candles flickered brightly, casting golden glow,
While festive hearts gathered, igniting the snow.
In the hush of the evening, our joy started to grow,
As music of laughter played soft and slow.

Under a blanket of stars, we shared all our dreams,
With warmth in our hearts, we flowed like the streams.
In this symphony silent, connected it seems,
As time stood still, lost in shimmering beams.

So let the cold linger, let the silence sing,
In the arms of togetherness, love is the spring.
For every soft heartbeat, the memories cling,
In a world made of magic, our spirits take wing.

## Twilight's Bitter Caress

In twilight's bitter caress, the colors collide,
As shadows grow longer, we stand side by side.
The air thick with magic that time cannot hide,
In this fleeting moment, our hopes coincide.

Fires crackled gently, casting warmth to the night,
While whispers of laughter danced in the light.
With every soft glance, the world felt so right,
As hearts swayed together, taking joyous flight.

Through twilight's embrace, we stumbled and spun,
In the glow of the embers, two souls become one.
The sweetness of memories just begun,
In the tapestry woven, our lives now are spun.

So cherish the night, let its magic unfold,
For in twilight's caress, our stories are told.
With memories woven like threads of pure gold,
In this charming embrace, our hearts never cold.

## The Chill Between Us

In the chill between us, the silence takes flight,
Yet warmth fills the air, a comforting sight.
In the space where we linger, love shines so bright,
As stars keep on twinkling, igniting the night.

With every soft glance, a spark starts to glow,
In whispers of laughter, sweet breezes will flow.
As we gather together 'neath blankets of snow,
The chill between us becomes passion's show.

Dancing in shadows, our hearts intertwined,
In the frost of the moment, two souls deeply aligned.
Through the cold winter night, our feelings defined,
In the warmth of connection, pure love we find.

So let the chill linger, let whispers enfold,
For in the dance of moments, our stories are told.
In the chill between us, our hearts are consoled,
In this festive embrace, a magic so bold.

## The Eternal Winter's Soliloquy

Snowflakes dance in the starry night,
Whispers of joy in the soft moonlight.
Fires crackle with warmth so bright,
Gather 'round, hearts intertwined tight.

Candles flicker, shadows play,
Throw your worries all away.
Laughter glows in the chill's embrace,
Together in this magical space.

Mittens clasped, hot cocoa in hand,
Stories shared, dreams beautifully planned.
Under the stars, we sing with cheer,
Winter's charm draws us all near.

Embrace the cold, the beauty it brings,
With every carol, our spirit sings.
In this moment, we find our way,
Eternal winter, forever we stay.

## Silent Sentinels of the Frost

Icicles shimmer, a diamond's kiss,
Nature's beauty in frosty bliss.
Trees stand tall in white cloaks of grace,
Guardians of memories in this space.

Soft whispers linger in every breeze,
Laughter echoes through frozen trees.
Children play in the fields of snow,
In this wonderland, joy starts to grow.

With sleds and dreams, we glide and soar,
Creating memories to cherish and adore.
Warm hearts gather, beneath twinkling lights,
Together we shine on these frigid nights.

So raise a glass in this frosty weather,
To friends and family, all together.
In the magic of winter, we revel and sing,
Silent sentinels, our hearts take wing.

## Winter's Silent Embrace

A crisp caress on the whispering air,
The world enchants, a beauty so rare.
Candles glow in each cozy nook,
In winter's embrace, all hearts are hooked.

Glistening snowflakes fall like dreams,
Illuminating the night with silver beams.
With every twinkle of starlit skies,
We gather warmth, our spirits rise.

Songs of old fill the frosty night,
Each note a spark of pure delight.
The laughter dances, the fire glows bright,
In winter's arms, everything feels right.

Together we craft this festive cheer,
Sharing stories to hold most dear.
In silence, we find our voices clear,
Winter's embrace, forever near.

## Echoes of the Icebound Night

In the hush of night, the world holds pause,
Frosted whispers, life's gentle cause.
Moonlight glimmers on the glistening ground,
Echoes of laughter and joy abound.

A chorus of joy, the carols ring,
Voices unite, each heart takes wing.
Candy canes and warm, sweet treats,
Under the stars, our spirit meets.

As the snow blankets the earth with grace,
Our footsteps paint a wondrous trace.
With fireside tales warming our feet,
In every moment, our hearts compete.

So let us celebrate this frozen night,
With thoughts of joy that feel so right.
Together we weave, our spirits bright,
In echoes of love, the icebound night.